Dear Theresa,

You will find enclosed just one example of the anticipated liability of Credit Card Companies who have perpetuated the financial scandal of our generation, namely; Collateralised Credit Exploitation (CCE) which is characterized as unwarranted entrapment which interminably indentures some of their best clients to long term financial slavery. This example serves to represent the 'Billions which will be repaid to Millions' due to Credit Card Companies cynical y and persistently exploiting vulnerable customers from whom they are reputed to gain 50% of their corporate profits. CCE has been established as carrying NO 'Value at Risk', NO Probability of Risk with an amount at risk of NIL but most tellingly where they have already been *repaid* their capital at up to 11x the original sum they still charge unwarranted, usurious and extortionate interest rates, fees and charges on their most vulnerable customers. Treating their BEST customers as 'can be abused junk accounts' when they are proven AAA+ is clearly & demonstrably 'fraudulently counterfactual'. The 'corporately designed' failure of Credit Card Companies to make a simple and generally accepted risk weighted calculation on CCE client credit cards (up to 1,151% positive return has been estimated) have been universally condemned as being unreasonable & exploitative.

How MUCH is ENOUGH!!!

Collateralised Credit Exploitation is practiced on AAA None Defaulting accounts & is in effect an Annuity in Perpetuity and is demonstrably Exploitative by Design -Extortionate by Intent - Fraudulent by Nature.

Our political & regulatory & financial establishment has demonstrated endogenously heterodoxical behaviour in their collective incapacity to respect the UK Citizen by ignoring the fact of and the damage caused by Collateralised Credit Exploitation.

Exploitative By Design - Extortionate By Intent - Fraudulent By Nature

Billions will be repaid to Millions' estimated cost to Credit Card Companies of Collateralised Credit Exploitation is conservatively put at between £50-75 Billion. Collateralised Credit Exploitation by Credit Card Companies is the cynical long term exploitation of vulnerable customers where there is no risk and no probability of risk to Credit Card Companies who perpetuate the practice.

One Example amongst millions, follows;

New Day Opus £ 110,000 gross on 10,000 @ 48.1% over 20 years*
New Day Marbles £ 84,000 gross on 9,000 @ 39.9% over 20 years*
Capital One £ 27,000 gross on 2.500 @ 31.1% over 20 years*
MBNA £ 76,000 gross on 8,000 @ 30.0% over 20 years*,
£ 46,000 gross on 5.000 @ 30.0% over 20 years*,
£ 12,000 gross on 3,000 @ 30.0% over 20 years*
BarclayCard £ 43,000 gross on 5.500 @ 26.5% over 20 years*
£ 20,000 gross on 3,000 @ 26.5% over 20 years*
RBS £ 85,000 gross on 14,000 @ 16.9% over 20 years*

£ **503,000 to be repaid** on £ **54,000**

*Each Credit Card to confirm exact extortion period & exploitative interest rate.

All amounts above are **PLUS** interest, charges, fees, fines & compensation conservatively creating a **£754.500** Collateralised Credit Exploitation Liability on 1) on six credit card companies (above) on 2) nine numbered cards over 20 exemplary years. Base Rate 0.25% to 0.50%. Credit Card Companies have been allowed to insidiously develop over time a purposefully distorted Credit Risk Analysis Model which effectively penalizes their best customers & imbalances the relationship between avaricious providers & vulnerable users of credit instruments. Collateralized Credit Exploitation clearly demonstrates that the 'Value at Risk' nexus does NOT exist for the Credit Card Company & that they are imposing unreasonable and extortionate charges onto the consumer. Rather than 'know' they are 'ignoring the rights & abasing the needs' of their customers.

Credit Card Companies have been allowed to insidiously develop over time a purposefully distorted Credit Risk Analysis Model which effectively penalizes their best customers and imbalances the relationship between avaricious providers & vulnerable users of credit instruments.

'Collateralized Credit Exploitation or CCE (Cynical Long Term Revolver Entrapment) is the scourge of our generation perpetrated with impunity by Credit Card Companies'

We have recently published our TimeOutCreditCards Exploitation Index (CCE Scandal Scenario) as follows: No.1 = No Counter Party Risk, No. 2 = Annuity in Perpetuity, No.3 = AAA None Defaulting, No.4 = PFI - PPI of which CCE is the greatest injustice, No.5 = Unregulated Financial Misconduct, No.6 = Unjustified Financial Exploitation, No.7 = Persistent Imperious Exploitation, No.8 = Abuse of any generally acceptable prudential regime, No 9 = Devoid of commonly accepted rationality or merit No. 10 = Fails any and every measure of financial risk based ethical behavior.

Interested parties across the world have now been invited to join the Movement @TimeOutCreditCards #PutAnEndToFinancialSlavery.

Several connected publications and keynote presentations are available T.V. Radio & Social, Business & Trade Media notified.

Legacy Societal Adverse Impacts & Abusive Effects - Just ONE Example

Principal (with 9 cards from 6 companies MBNA, Capital One, RBS, BarclayCard, New Day Opus & Marbles) £ 54,000 Amount Repaid (estimated over 20 years) £ 503.000. 9 x Credit Cards from 6 Credit Card Companies interest up to 48.1% (base rate 0.25% to 0.50%). Risk Weighted Asset - up to 1,151% positive return. After almost 20 years as an impeccable payer our borrower asked politely over a period of time (2013 - 2018) 9 Credit Card companies to reduce their high rates of up to 48%+ so that they could be paid off, ALL REFUSED !!!

Repayment of those 9 cards on a principal amount of £ 54,000will have up to 20 years incur estimated gross payments of £ 503,000 (each credit card company has been asked to provide accurate payment amounts or engage in constructive discussion with the payee but each has effectively declined to do so) No financial organization has the right to impose a combination of excessive and unwarranted interest + charges + punitive fees on nominal amounts that cannot be paid back within an individual's lifetime by creating sustained (Collateralized Credit Exploitation) CCEs at rates which are not supported by any rational, reasonable, ethical measure or by any accepted financial risk ratios or prudential regime.

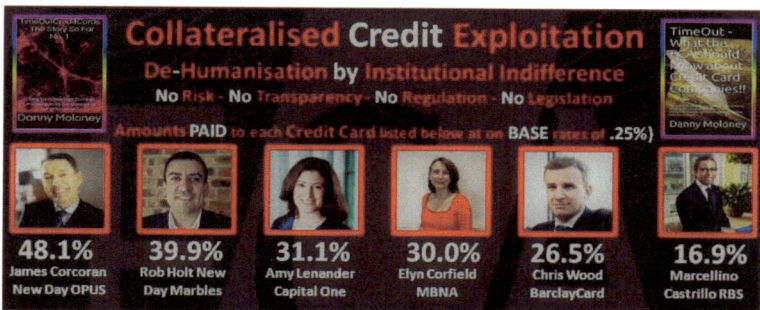

De Humanization by Institutional Indifference

Principal - £54,000   Estimated Amount Repaid** - £503,000
Over Length of Time* - 0 to 20 years
Credit Card Interest – up to 48.1%
Bank of England Base Rate – 0.25 % to 0.50%

Amount to be repaid by the Credit Card Companies
Principal + OverPayment + Interest + Charges + Compensation =
£ 503.000*** (estimate)
Status - Creditor of each credit card named above

CCE Value at Risk (VaR) Time Frame - Lifetime, Amount at Risk - NIL, Probability of Risk - NIL, Collateralized Credit Exploitation is cynical long term entrapment & unconscionable financial slavery where there is No Risk - No Transparency - No Regulation - No Legislation.

*Each Credit Card Company have to date withheld the necessary information to make an accurate calculation of total payments made ** Each Credit Card Company can provide a more detailed breakdown. *** Projection. Account Number for 9 x cards ending (available)

How MUCH is ENOUGH!!!

Collateralised Credit Exploitation is practiced on AAA None Defaulting accounts & is in effect an Annuity in Perpetuity and is demonstrably Exploitative by Design -Extortionate by Intent - Fraudulent by Nature.

Our political & regulatory & financial establishment has demonstrated endogenously heterodoxical behaviour in their collective incapacity to respect the UK Citizen by ignoring the fact of and the damage caused by Collateralised Credit Exploitation.

Danny Moloney, MBA, MSc, MA, MAPCE, MACT (DBA IP).
Greater Eccles, Manchester, United Kingdom.
Sunday 8th July 2018

Find Out More On: @TimeOutCCards and/or @DisCreditCards *and/or* TimeOutCreditCards – The Story So Far - No.1 https://www.amazon.co.uk/dp/B01N393PDI *and/or* What The FCA Should Know About Credit Cards https://www.amazon.co.uk/dp/B073Z1YVNT and/or Chronolog 'Talk To Us, Prime Minister'

Breaking Free of the Shackles of Financial Slavery

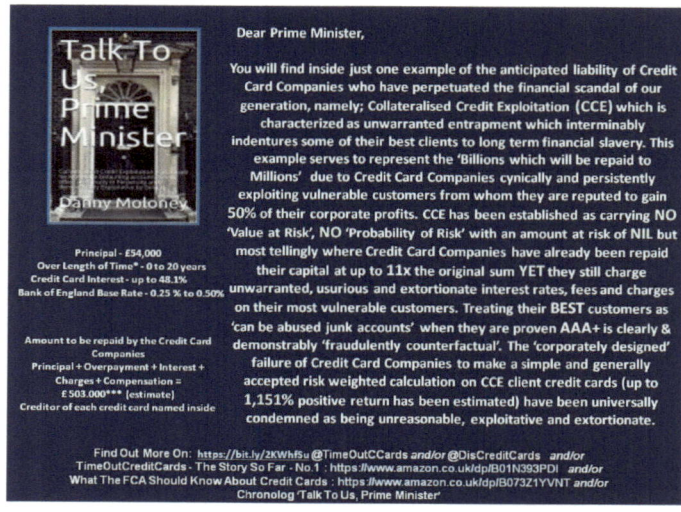

Talk to us, Prime Minister

Letter One 15th April 2018 - Theresa May

124 Peel Green Road, Eccles, Manchester, M30 7AZ, U.K.
Telephone: 0161 789 8787   Email: timeoutcreditcards@globalmehpte.com

Mrs. Theresa May,
10 Downing Street,
Westminster
London,
SW 1A 2AA

Theresa May - 1

April 15th 2018

'The financialisation of our economy has rendered political institutions virtually powerless to represent the interests of UK consumers'.

Dear Mrs. May,

I write on this occasion to represent millions of U.K. citizens, who daily labor under the insidious burden of Collateralised Credit Exploitation (a perversely distorted and financially reprehensible loan to payment ratio) perpetrated by the named Credit Card Companies and tacitly supported by the Government Bodies, Authorities & Associations, also named below.

Andrew Bailey at the FCA has attempted to deal with the scandal by addressing 'Persistent Debt' but the real issue is 'Persistent Exploitation' by unregulated Credit Card Companies.

Credit Card Companies - The Perpetrators

MBNA - Elyn Corfield ,   OPUS - James Corcoran,   MARBLES - Rob Holt,   Royal Bank of Scotland - Marcellino Castrillo,   Capital One - Amy Lenander,   Barclaycard - Chris Wood

Government Bodies & Authorities & Associations - The Regulators

Financial Ombudsman - Caroline Wayman, Prudential Regulation Authority - Mark Carney, Competition & Markets Authority - Andrea Coscelli, Payment Systems Regulator - Hannah Nixon, Philip Hammond - Chancellor of the Exchequer, Andrew Bailey - Financial Conduct

Authority, UK Cards Association - Graham Peacop, Finance & Leasing Association - Richard Jones, British Bankers Association - Eric Leenders, Lending & Standards - Board Dave Pickering & Money Advice Service - Charles Counsell.

I would like you to invite those named above to meet with you and I at 10 Downing Street, the seat of our executive government to answer the questions from myself, 1) Why the Credit Card Companies & the Government Bodies & Authorities have behaved like this and effectively allowed this scandal to persist & from you; 2) What are they going to do about it?

Thanks for your support in resolving this demonstrable and injurious evil within our society.

Danny Moloney
Greater Eccles, Manchester, United Kingdom

Overleaf is an example of Collateralised Credit Exploitation about which all of the above named has been informed about and ignored to date. Principal (with 9 cards from 6 companies) **£ 60.799** Amount Repaid (estimated over 20 years) **£ 472.001** Amount which will be Repaid (estimated over 30 years) **£ 699.933**. 9 x Credit Cards from 6 Credit Card Companies interest up to 48.1% Risk Weighted Asset - up to **1,151%** positive return

After almost 20 years as an impeccable payer our borrower asked politely over a period of time (2013 - 2017) 9 Credit Card companies to reduce their high rates of up to 48%+ so that they could be paid off, ALL REFUSED !!!

Repayment of those 9 cards on a principal amount of £ 60,799 will have up to 20 years incur estimated gross payments of £ 472,001 and over 30 years will incur estimated gross payments of £ 699,933 (each credit card company has been asked to provide accurate payment amounts or engagement in constructive discussion with the payee but each has effectively declined to do so) No financial organization has the right to impose a combination of excessive and unwarranted interest + charges + punitive fees on nominal amounts that cannot be paid back within an individual's lifetime by creating sustained (Collateralized Credit Exploitation) CCEs at rates which are not supported by any rational, reasonable, ethical measure or by any accepted financial risk ratios or prudential regime.

Synopsis of Submission to the Financial Conduct Authority (FCA) Collective Amount May 2017

NINE Card Accounts with **SIX x Credit Cards Companies** (named overleaf)

Principal - **£60,799**

Estimated Amount Repaid** - **£472,001**   Over Length of Time* - **0** to **30 years**
Credit Card Interest – up to **48.1%**   Bank of England Base Rate - **0.50%**

Repayment Record - **Excellent**   Creditworthiness – **AAA +** (treated as CCC)
Approach Made to each Credit Card Company - **Yes**   Approach Rebuffed - **Yes**

Good Customer Exploitation Index Score - **10**   (Ethical Behavior & Practices CODEX)
(Where **0** is very good and **10** is very bad)

Toxic Financial Practices Score - **10**   (Unethical Ethical Behavior & Practices INDEX)
(Where **0** is very good and **10** is very bad)

Credit, Market or Operational Risk Score - **0%**   (Discredit Index (DSCI)
(Where **0%** is no risk and **100%** is extreme risk)

Counter Party Rating - **AAA**   External Analysis Report - Negative

Risk Weighted Asset - **+ 1,151%** positive return
Risk Weighted Calculation - **Unreasonable** & **Exploitative**

Governmental and/or Regulatory and/or Supervisory Review
Unknown and/or **Ineffective** and/or **Inadequate**

Prime Indicators - **Person Backed Security** (PBS)   Financial Scandal Potential - **High**
Business Practices - **Questionable**   Corporate Behavior - **Questionable**

Amount to be repaid

Principal + OverPayment + Interest + Charges + Compensation = £ 350,403.00***

(estimate)

Status - Creditor of each credit card named above.

*Each Credit Card Company have to date withheld the necessary information to make an accurate calculation of total payments made ** Each Credit Card Company can provide a more detailed breakdown. *** Projection. Account for cards ending (available)

[TimeOutCreditCards 1](#) (Published 27th January 2017)

TimeOutCreditCards 2 - Credit Card Companies Exposed
(To Be Published on FCA Aftermath)
TimeOutCreditCards 3 - The Regulators - Held to Account
(To Be Published on FCA Aftermath)
TimeOutCreditCards 4 - The Investigation Credit On Trial
(To Be Published on FCA Aftermath)
TimeOutCreditCards 5 - The Legislation - Parliament under Scrutiny
(To Be Published on FCA Aftermath)
TimeOutCreditCards 6 - Financial, Governmental Establishment Nexus
(To Be Published on FCA Aftermath)
TimeOutCreditCards 7 - The Insouciant Aura of Financial Privilege
(To Be Published on FCA Aftermath)

TimeOutCreditCards Exploitation Index: Definition **No.**1 = No Counter Party Risk, Definition **No.**2 = Annuity in Perpetuity, Definition **No.**3 = AAA None Defaulting, Definition **No.**4 = PFI - PPI – CCE, Definition **No.**5 = Unregulated Financial Misconduct, Definition **No.**6 = Unjustified Financial Exploitation

Letter Two 14th May 2018 - Theresa May

Greater Eccles, Manchester, M30 7AZ, U.K.
Telephone: 0161 789 8787   Email: timeoutcreditcards@globalmehpte.com

Mrs. Theresa May,   Theresa May - 2
10 Downing Street,
Westminster
London,
SW 1A 2AA   Monday 14th May 2018

'Collateralised Credit Exploitation or CCE (Cynical Long Term Revolver Entrapment)
is the scourge of our generation perpetrated with impunity by Credit Card Companies'

Dear Mrs. May,

Further to our letter to you of Sunday 15/4/18, to which we await your reply.

We have recently published our **TimeOutCreditCards Exploitation Index** (CCE Scandal Scenario) as follows: **No.**1 = No Counter Party Risk, **No.** 2 = Annuity in Perpetuity, **No.**3 = AAA None Defaulting, **No.**4 = PFI - PPI of which CCE is the greatest injustice, **No.5** = Unregulated Financial Misconduct, **No.**6 = Unjustified Financial Exploitation, **No.7** = Persistent Impunious Exploitation, **No.8** = Abuse of any generally acceptable prudential regime, **No 9** = Devoid of commonly accepted rationality or merit **No. 10** = Fails any and every measure of financial risk based ethical behaviour.

Interested parties across the world have now been invited to join the Movement @TimeOutCreditCards #PutAnEndToFinancialSlavery. Several connected publications and keynote presentations are available T.V. Radio & Social, Business & Trade Media notified.

Thank you for your support in resolving this demonstrable, injurious, flagrant and persistent financial slavery within our society.

Danny Moloney
Restitutional Activist
Greater Eccles, Manchester, United Kingdom

Legacy Societal Adverse Impacts & Abusive Effects - Just ONE Example

Principal (with 9 cards from 6 companies MBNA, Capital One, RBS, BarclayCard, New Day Opus & Marbles)) **£ 60.799** Amount Repaid (estimated over 20 years) **£ 472.001** Amount which will be Repaid (estimated over 30 years) **£ 699.933.** 9 x Credit Cards from 6 Credit Card Companies interest up to 48.1% (base rate 0.25% to 0.50%) Risk Weighted Asset - up to **1,151%** positive return. After almost 20 years as an impeccable payer our borrower asked politely over a period of time (2013 - 2017) 9 Credit Card companies to reduce their high rates of up to 48%+ so that they could be paid off, **ALL REFUSED !!!**

Repayment of those 9 cards on a principal amount of £ 60,799 will have up to 20 years incur estimated gross payments of £ 472,001 and over 30 years will incur estimated gross payments of £ 699,933 (each credit card company has been asked to provide accurate payment amounts or engage in constructive discussion with the payee but each has effectively declined to do so) No financial organization has the right to impose a combination of excessive and unwarranted interest + charges + punitive fees on nominal amounts that cannot be paid back within an individual's lifetime by creating sustained (Collateralized Credit Exploitation) CCEs at rates which are not supported by any rational, reasonable, ethical measure or by any accepted financial risk ratios or prudential regime.

Principal - **£60,799**
Estimated Amount Repaid** - **£472,001**
Over Length of Time* - **0** to **20 years**
Credit Card Interest – up to **48.1%**
Bank of England Base Rate – 0.25 % to **0.50%**

Amount to be repaid by the Credit Card Companies
Principal + OverPayment + Interest + Charges + Compensation = £ 350,403.00***

(estimate)

Status - Creditor of each credit card named above.

*Each Credit Card Company have to date withheld the necessary information to make an accurate calculation of total payments made ** Each Credit Card Company can provide a more detailed breakdown. *** Projection. Account for 9 x cards ending (available)

Letter Three 20th June 2018 - Theresa May

Greater Eccles, Manchester, M30 7AZ, U.K.

Telephone: 0161 789 8787   Email: timeoutcreditcards@globalmehpte.com

Mrs. Theresa May,   Theresa May - 3
10 Downing Street,
Westminster
London,
SW 1A 2AA   Wednesday 20h June 2018

Billions will be repaid to Millions of UK Consumers

Dear Mrs. May,

Further to our letters to you of 15/4/18 & 14/5/18, to which we await your reply.

We look forward to the Collateralised Credit Exploitation Summit to be held at Downing Street, which will be followed by presentations across the country entitled 'Ending Financial Slavery to Credit Card Companies'.

Thank you for your support in resolving this demonstrable, injurious, flagrant and persistent financial evil within our society.

Danny Moloney
Restitutional Activist
Greater Eccles, Manchester, United Kingdom

Legacy Societal Adverse Impacts & Abusive Effects - Just ONE Example

We have recently published our **TimeOutCreditCards Exploitation Index** (CCE Scandal Scenario) as follows: **No.**1 = No Counter Party Risk, **No.** 2 = Annuity in Perpetuity, **No.**3 = AAA None Defaulting, **No.**4 = PFI - PPI of which CCE is the greatest injustice, **No.**5 = Unregulated Financial Misconduct, **No.**6 = Unjustified Financial Exploitation, **No.**7 = Persistent Impunious Exploitation, **No.**8 = Abuse of any generally acceptable prudential regime, **No 9** = Devoid of commonly accepted rationality or merit **No. 10** = Fails any and every measure of financial risk based ethical behaviour.

Principal (with 9 cards from 6 companies MBNA, Capital One, RBS, BarclayCard, New Day Opus & Marbles)) **£ 60.799** Amount Repaid (estimated over 20 years) **£ 472.001** Amount which will be Repaid (estimated over 30 years) **£ 699.933.** 9 x Credit Cards from 6 Credit Card Companies interest up to 48.1% (base rate 0.25% to 0.50%) Risk Weighted Asset - up to **1,151%** positive return. After almost 20 years as an impeccable payer our borrower asked politely over a period of time (2013 - 2017) 9 Credit Card companies to reduce their high rates of up to 48%+ so that they could be paid off, **ALL REFUSED !!!**

Repayment of those 9 cards on a principal amount of £ 60,799 will have up to 20 years incur estimated gross payments of £ 472,001 and over 30 years will incur estimated gross payments of £ 699,933 (each credit card company has been asked to provide accurate payment amounts or engage in constructive discussion with the payee but each has effectively declined to do so) No financial organization has the right to impose a combination of excessive and unwarranted interest + charges + punitive fees on nominal amounts that cannot be paid back within an individual's lifetime by creating sustained (Collateralized Credit Exploitation) CCEs at rates which are not supported by any rational, reasonable, ethical measure or by any accepted financial risk ratios or prudential regime.

Principal - **£60,799**   Estimated Amount Repaid** - **£472,001**

Over Length of Time* - **0** to **20 years**

Credit Card Interest – up to **48.1%**

Bank of England Base Rate – 0.25 % to **0.50%**

Amount to be repaid by the Credit Card Companies

Principal + OverPayment + Interest + Charges + Compensation = £ 350,403.00***

(estimate)

Status - Creditor of each credit card named above.

*Each Credit Card Company have to date withheld the necessary information to make an accurate calculation of total payments made ** Each Credit Card Company can provide a more detailed breakdown. *** Projection. Account for 9 x cards ending (available)

Letter Four 26th June 2018 - Theresa May

Greater Eccles, Manchester, M30 7AZ, U.K.

Telephone: + 44 161 789 8787   Email: timeoutcreditcards@globalmehpte.com

Mrs. Theresa May,
10 Downing Street,
Westminster
London,
SW 1A 2AA

Theresa May - 4

Tuesday 26[h] June 2018

Billions will be repaid to Millions of UK Consumers

Dear Mrs. May,

Further to our letters to you of 15/4/18 & 14/5/18 & 20/6/18 to which we await your reply.

We attach overleaf a letter sent today to Chris Smerdon, Head of Customer Assistance at MBNA.

Thank you for your support in resolving this demonstrable, injurious, flagrant and persistent financial evil within our society.

Danny Moloney
Restitutional Activist
Greater Eccles, Manchester, United Kingdom

Legacy Societal Adverse Impacts & Abusive Effects - Just ONE Example

We have recently published our **TimeOutCreditCards Exploitation Index** (CCE Scandal Scenario) as follows: **No.**1 = No Counter Party Risk, **No.** 2 = Annuity in Perpetuity, **No.**3 = AAA None Defaulting, **No.**4 = PFI - PPI of which CCE is the greatest injustice, **No.**5 = Unregulated Financial Misconduct, **No.**6 = Unjustified Financial Exploitation, **No.**7 = Persistent Impunious Exploitation, **No.**8 = Abuse of any generally acceptable prudential regime, **No 9** = Devoid of commonly accepted rationality or merit **No. 10** = Fails any and every measure of financial risk based ethical behaviour.

Principal (with 9 cards from 6 companies MBNA, Capital One, RBS, BarclayCard, New Day Opus & Marbles)) **£ 60.799** Amount Repaid (estimated over 20 years) **£ 472.001** Amount which will be Repaid (estimated over 30 years) **£ 699.933**. 9 x Credit Cards from 6 Credit Card Companies interest up to 48.1% (base rate 0.25% to 0.50%) Risk Weighted Asset - up to **1,151%** positive return. After almost 20 years as an impeccable payer our borrower asked politely over a period of time (2013 - 2017) 9 Credit Card companies to reduce their high rates of up to 48%+ so that they could be paid off, **ALL REFUSED !!!**

Repayment of those 9 cards on a principal amount of £ 60,799 will have up to 20 years incur estimated gross payments of £ 472,001 and over 30 years will incur estimated gross payments of £ 699,933 (each credit card company has been asked to provide accurate payment amounts or engage in constructive discussion with the payee but each has effectively declined to do so)

No financial organization has the right to impose a combination of excessive and unwarranted interest + charges + punitive fees on nominal amounts that cannot be paid back within an individual's lifetime by creating sustained (Collateralized Credit Exploitation) CCEs at rates which are not supported by any rational, reasonable, ethical measure or by any accepted financial risk ratios or prudential regime.

Principal - **£60,799**   Estimated Amount Repaid** - **£472,001**
Over Length of Time* - **0** to **20 years**
Credit Card Interest – up to **48.1%**
Bank of England Base Rate – 0.25 % to **0.50%**

Amount to be repaid by the Credit Card Companies
Principal + OverPayment + Interest + Charges + Compensation = £ 350,403.00***
(estimate)

Status - Creditor of each credit card named above.

*Each Credit Card Company have to date withheld the necessary information to make an accurate calculation of total payments made ** Each Credit Card Company can provide a more detailed breakdown. *** Projection. Account for 9 x cards ending (available)

Greater Eccles, Manchester, M30 7AZ
Telephone - + 44 161 789 8787   e-mail timeoutcreditcards@globalmehpte.com

Chris Smerdon	Chris - 1
MBNA Ltd	MBNA Card Nos. ending 7548/3819/0756
Chester Business Park,	Your ref: LL 014 16235 0000Y47 05128 31
Wrexham Road	MBNA 12 - 1997 - 2007 - 2017 - 2027
Chester, CH4 9FB	Tuesday 26th June 2018

It is TimeOutCreditCards, our society will never support the patently amoral behaviour of Credit Card Companies. When they treat their best / most loyal / immensely profitable & interminably indentured customers with such disdain. They clearly have no moral imperative to behave responsibly creating as they have an impenetrable & immoral institutional indifference to normally acceptable financial practice via their endemic & cynical use of long term entrapment Collateralised Credit Exploitation, which carries No Counter Party Risk - Annuity in Perpetuity - AAA None Defaulting - No Transparency - No Regulation - No Legislation

Dear Chris,

In your letter of 14th June 2018, you claim £ **242.64** from us when in fact MBNA 'owe' to us the following on cards ending 7548 = £ **25,921**, 3819 = £ **42,415**, 0756 = £ **12,000** (making a conservative total of £80,336 being made up of net principal, overpayment, interest and charges) a conservative estimate where your own reasonable profit has been pre-deducted (the actual figures owed are much larger). This letter has been forwarded for comment and action to Elyn Corfield CEO of MBNA (who has corporate responsibility), Theresa May Conservative Prime Minister who together with Jeremy Corbyn Labour Opposition Leader (have legislatory responsibility) and Andrew Bailey CEO of the FCA who has regulatory responsibility) for the cynical and persistent Collateralized Credit Exploitation by MBNA

Danny Moloney
Greater Eccles, Manchester.

Principal - **£19,250**
Estimated Amount Repaid* - **£80,336**
Over Length of Time** - **0 to 20 years**
Credit Card Interest - **30.1+%**
Bank of England Base Rate - 0.25 % to **0.50%**

Amount to be repaid by MBNA (on cards ending 7548 - 3819 - 0756)
Principal + OverPayment + Interest + Charges + Compensation = £ 80,336.00* (estimate)

*MBNA have to date withheld the necessary information to make an accurate calculation of total payments made ** MBNA can provide a more detailed breakdown.
*** Projection. Account for 3 x cards ending (available)

After almost 20 years as an impeccable payer our borrower asked politely over a period of time (2013 - 2018) MBNA to reduce their high rates of up to 30+%+ so that they could be paid off,
ALL REFUSED !!!

No financial organization has the right to impose a combination of excessive and unwarranted interest + charges + punitive fees on nominal amounts that cannot be paid back within an individual's lifetime by creating sustained (Collateralized Credit Exploitation) CCEs at rates which are not supported by any rational, reasonable, ethical measure or by any accepted financial risk ratios or prudential regime.

Billions will be repaid to Millions of UK Consumers
Collateralized Credit Exploitation Condemnation - Regulation - Legislation

TimeOutCreditCards Exploitation Index for **MBNA** (CCE Scandal Scenario) **No.1** = No Counter Party Risk, **No. 2** = Annuity in Perpetuity, **No.3** = AAA None Defaulting, **No.4** = PFI - PPI of which CCE is the greatest injustice, **No.5** = Unregulated Financial Misconduct, **No.6** = Unjustified Financial Exploitation, **No.7** = Persistent Impunious Exploitation, **No.8** = Abuse of any generally acceptable prudential regime, **No 9** = Devoid of commonly accepted rationality or merit **No. 10** = Fails any and every measure of financial risk based ethical behaviour.

Letter Five 3rd July 2018 – Theresa May

Greater Eccles, Manchester, M30 7AZ, U.K.

Telephone: + 44 161 789 8787   Email: timeoutcreditcards@globalmehpte.com

Mrs. Theresa May,   Theresa May - 5
10 Downing Street,
Westminster
London,
SW 1A 2AA   Tuesday 3rd July 2018

Dear Theresa,

Billions will be repaid to Millions of UK Consumers

Further to our letters to you of 15/4/18 & 14/5/18 & 20/6/18 to which we await your reply.

We attach overleaf a letter sent today to Francesca Rae of New Day - OPUS

Thank you for your support in resolving this demonstrable, injurious, flagrant and persistent financial evil within our society.

Danny Moloney
Restitutional Activist
Greater Eccles, Manchester, United Kingdom

Legacy Societal Adverse Impacts & Abusive Effects - Just ONE Example

We have recently published our **TimeOutCreditCards Exploitation Index** (CCE Scandal Scenario) as follows: **No.**1 = No Counter Party Risk, **No.** 2 = Annuity in Perpetuity, **No.**3 = AAA None Defaulting, **No.**4 = PFI - PPI of which CCE is the greatest injustice, **No.5** = Unregulated Financial Misconduct, **No.**6 = Unjustified Financial Exploitation, **No.7** = Persistent Impunious

Exploitation, **No.8** = Abuse of any generally acceptable prudential regime, **No 9** = Devoid of commonly accepted rationality or merit **No. 10** = Fails any and every measure of financial risk based ethical behaviour.

Principal (with 9 cards from 6 companies MBNA, Capital One, RBS, BarclayCard, New Day Opus & Marbles)) **£ 54,000.** Amount Repaid (estimated over 20 years) **£ 503,000** Amount which will be Repaid (estimated over 30 years) **£ 699.933+.** 9 x Credit Cards from 6 Credit Card Companies interest up to 48.1% (base rate 0.25% to 0.50%) Risk Weighted Asset - up to **1,151%** positive return. After almost 20 years as an impeccable payer our borrower asked politely over a period of time (2013 - 2017) 9 Credit Card companies to reduce their high rates of up to 48%+ so that they could be paid off, **ALL REFUSED !!!**

Repayment of those 9 cards on a principal amount of £ 60,799 will have up to 20 years incur estimated gross payments of £ 472,001 and over 30 years will incur estimated gross payments of £ 699,933 (each credit card company has been asked to provide accurate payment amounts or engage in constructive discussion with the payee but each has effectively declined to do so) No financial organization has the right to impose a combination of excessive and unwarranted interest + charges + punitive fees on nominal amounts that cannot be paid back within an individual's lifetime by creating sustained (Collateralized Credit Exploitation) CCEs at rates which are not supported by any rational, reasonable, ethical measure or by any accepted financial risk ratios or prudential regime.

Principal - **£54,000**
Estimated Amount Repaid** - **£503,000**
Over Length of Time* - **0** to **20 years**
Credit Card Interest - up to **48.1%**
Bank of England Base Rate - 0.25 % to **0.50%**

Amount to be repaid by the Credit Card Companies
Principal + OverPayment + Interest + Charges + Compensation = £ 503,000* (estimate)

Status - Creditor of each credit card named above.

*Each Credit Card Company have to date withheld the necessary information to make an accurate calculation of total payments made ** Each Credit Card Company can provide a more detailed breakdown. *** Projection. Account for 9 x cards ending (available)

Greater Eccles, Manchester, M30 7AZ

Telephone - + 44 161 789 8787   e-mail timeoutcreditcards@globalmehpte.com

Francesca Rae   Opus Card No. ending 5570
OPUS   Your Ref: 00011050000001489808
P. O. Box 136   OPUS **13** - 1997 - 2007 - 2017 – 2027
Sheffield,
S98 IHB   Tuesday 3rd July 2018

It is TimeOutCreditCards, our society will never support the patently amoral behaviour of Credit Card Companies. When they treat their best / most loyal / immensely profitable & interminably indentured customers with such disdain. They clearly have no moral imperative to behave responsibly creating as they have an impenetrable & immoral institutional indifference to normally acceptable financial practice via their endemic & cynical use of long term entrapment Collateralised Credit Exploitation, which carries No Counter Party Risk – An Annuity in Perpetuity - AAA None Defaulting - No Transparency - No Regulation - No Legislation

Dear Francesca,

In response to your letter of 25th June 2018, we confirm that New Day - OPUS 'owe' to us on the following card ending 5570 = £ **110,000** (being a conservative subtotal and made up of net principal, overpayment, interest and charges); compensation to be calculated.

This letter has been forwarded for comment & action to James Corcoran CEO of OPUS (who has corporate responsibility), Theresa May Conservative Prime Minister who together with Jeremy Corbyn Labour Opposition Leader (have legislatory responsibility) & Andrew Bailey CEO of the FCA who has regulatory responsibility) for the cynical & persistent Collateralized Credit Exploitation practiced by New Day - OPUS.

Danny Moloney
Greater Eccles, Manchester.

Principal - **£9,692**   Estimated Amount Repaid* - **£110,000**
Over Length of Time** - **0** to **20 years**
Credit Card Interest - **48.1+%**
Bank of England Base Rate - 0.25 % to **0.50%**

Amount to be repaid by New Day – OPUS (on card ending 5570)
Principal + OverPayment + Interest + Charges + Compensation = £ 110,000 *** (estimate)

*OPUS have to date withheld the necessary information to make an accurate calculation of total payments made ** OPUS (+ predecessors) can provide a more detailed breakdown. *** Projection. Account for 1 x cards ending (5570)

After almost 20 years as an impeccable payer (incl previous credit provider) our borrower asked politely over a period of time (2013 - 2018) OPUS to reduce their high and extortionate rates of up to 48+%+ so that they could be paid off, **ALL REFUSED !!!**

No financial organization has the right to impose a combination of excessive and unwarranted interest + charges + punitive fees on nominal amounts that cannot be paid back within an individual's lifetime by creating sustained (Collateralized Credit Exploitation) CCEs at rates which are not supported by any rational, reasonable, ethical measure or by any accepted financial risk ratios or prudential regime.

Billions will be repaid to Millions of UK Consumers
Collateralized Credit Exploitation Condemnation - Regulation - Legislation

TimeOutCreditCards Exploitation Index for **OPUS** (CCE Scandal Scenario) **No.1** = No Counter Party Risk, **No. 2** = Annuity in Perpetuity, **No.3** = AAA None Defaulting, **No.4** = PFI - PPI of which CCE is the greatest injustice, **No.5** = Unregulated Financial Misconduct, **No.6** = Unjustified Financial Exploitation, **No.7** = Persistent Impunious Exploitation, **No.8** = Abuse of any generally acceptable prudential regime, **No 9** = Devoid of commonly accepted rationality or merit **No. 10** = Fails any and every measure of financial risk based ethical behaviour.

Letter Six 9th July 2018 – Theresa May

Greater Eccles, Manchester, M30 7AZ, U.K.
Telephone: + 44 161 789 8787   Email: timeoutcreditcards@globalmehpte.com

Mrs. Theresa May,   Theresa May - 6
10 Downing Street,
Westminster
London,
SW 1A 2AA   Monday 9th July 2018

Dear Theresa,

You will find overleaf just one example of the anticipated liability of Credit Card Companies who have perpetuated the financial scandal of our generation, namely; Collateralised Credit Exploitation (CCE) which is characterized as unwarranted entrapment which interminably indentures some of their best clients to long term financial slavery. This example serves to represent the 'Billions which will be repaid to Millions' due to Credit Card Companies cynically and persistently exploiting vulnerable customers from whom they are reputed to gain 50% of their corporate profits. CCE has been established as carrying **NO** 'Value at Risk', **NO** 'Probability of Risk' with an amount at risk of **NIL** but most tellingly where they have already been *repaid* their capital at up to **11x** the original sum they still charge unwarranted, usurious and extortionate interest rates, fees and charges on their most vulnerable customers. Treating their BEST customers as 'can be abused junk accounts' when they are proven AAA+ is clearly & demonstrably 'fraudulently counterfactual'. The 'corporately designed' failure of Credit Card Companies to make a simple and generally accepted risk weighted calculation on CCE client credit cards (up to 1,151% positive return has been estimated) have been universally condemned as being unreasonable & exploitative.

How MUCH is ENOUGH!!!

Collateralised Credit Exploitation is practiced on AAA None Defaulting accounts & is in effect an Annuity in Perpetuity and is demonstrably Exploitative by Design -Extortionate by Intent - Fraudulent by Nature.

Our political & regulatory & financial establishment has demonstrated endogenously heterodoxical behaviour in their collective incapacity to respect the UK Citizen by ignoring the fact of and the damage caused by Collateralised Credit Exploitation.

Danny Moloney,
MBA, MSc, MA, MAPCE, MACT (DBA IP).
Greater Eccles, Manchester, United Kingdom.
Sunday 8th July 2018

Exploitative By Design - Extortionate By Intent - Fraudulent By Nature
Billions will be repaid to Millions' estimated cost to Credit Card Companies of Collateralised Credit Exploitation is conservatively put at between £50-75 Billion. Collateralised Credit Exploitation by Credit Card Companies is the cynical long term exploitation of vulnerable customers where there is no risk and no probability of risk to Credit Card Companies who perpetuate the practice.

One Example amongst millions, follows;
*Each Credit Card to confirm exact extortion period & exploitative interest rate.
New Day Opus £ 110,000 gross on 10,000 @ 48.1% over 20 years*
New Day Marbles £ 84,000 gross on 9,000 @ 39.9% over 20 years*
Capital One £ 27,000 gross on 2.500 @ 31.1% over 20 years*

MBNA £ 76,000 gross on 8,000 @ 30.0% over 20 years*,
£ 46,000 gross on 5.000 @ 30.0% over 20 years*,
£ 12,000 gross on 3,000 @ 30.0% over 20 years*
BarclayCard £ 43,000 gross on 5.500 @ 26.5% over 20 years*

£ 20,000 gross on 3,000 @ 26.5% over 20 years*
RBS £ 85,000 gross on 14,000 @ 16.9% over 20 years*

£ **503,000** to be repaid on £ **54,000**

All amounts above are **PLUS** interest, charges, fees, fines & compensation conservatively creating a £**754.500** Collateralised Credit Exploitation Liability on 1) on six credit card companies (above) on 2) nine numbered cards over 20 exemplary years. Base Rate 0.25% to 0.50%. Credit Card Companies have been allowed to insidiously develop over time a purposefully distorted Credit Risk Analysis Model which effectively penalizes their best customers & imbalances the relationship between avaricious providers & vulnerable users of credit instruments. Collateralized Credit Exploitation clearly demonstrates that the 'Value at Risk' nexus does NOT exist for the Credit Card Company & that they are imposing unreasonable and extortionate charges onto the consumer. Rather than 'know' they are 'ignoring the rights & abasing the needs' of their customers. Credit Card Companies have been allowed to insidiously develop over time a purposefully distorted Credit Risk Analysis Model which effectively penalizes their best customers and imbalances the relationship between avaricious providers & vulnerable users of credit instruments.

Find Out More On: https://bit.ly/2KWhfSu *and/or*
@TimeOutCCards and/or @DisCreditCards *and/or*
TimeOutCreditCards – The Story So Far - No.1 *and/or*
https://www.amazon.co.uk/dp/B01N393PDI *and/or*
What The FCA Should Know About Credit Cards https://www.amazon.co.uk/dp/B073Z1YVNT
and/or Chronolog 'Talk To Us, Prime Minister'

TimeOutCreditCards

Collateralised Credit Exploitation

New Day Opus - New Day Marbles - Capital One - MBNA - Barclaycard - RBS

Your MOST profitable customers have rights too for Justice and Respect.

It is no surprise that James Corcoran of New Day Opus, Rob Holt of New Day Marbles, Amy Lenander of Capital One, Elyn Corfield of MBNA, Chris Wood of BarclayCard & Marcellino Castrillo of Royal Bank of Scotland, have not responded to letters sent to each one of them personally and provided a personalized response by way of explanation as to their collective behavior in perpetrating the financial scandal of our generation - Collateralized Credit Exploitation.

TimeOutCreditCards Collateralised Credit Exploitation has impaired the inherent right of individual or collective customers for equitable financial management.

If Politicians - Regulators - Credit Card Companies fail to support the best interests of a member of the public; they are entitled to take the measures necessary to maintain respect and bring an end to exploitation exemplified by TimeOutCreditCards Collateralised Credit Exploitation, which has been proven to be Credit Exploitation & Financial Slavery.

Customers are equally entitled to a level of support which should be designed and is subsequently conducted in accordance with recognized best practice and ethical standards.

Customers have the right to expect Politicians - Regulators to use commonly accepted standards commonly assess, confirm and improve their governance and financial management policies and practice and be accountable to their customers for their malpractice.

Politicians - Regulators have implicit responsibility to protect and safeguard customers from extortion by unregulated Credit Card Companies.

Collateralised Credit Exploitation is a clear case of financial exploitation, it was the very scenario that the Legislatory & Regulatory framework has been designed to confront, challenge, manage & control in the interests of consumers.

'No financial organization has the right to make excessive interest & charges on nominal amounts that cannot be paid back within an individual's lifetime by creating (Collateralised Credit Exploitation) CCEs'

""'It should be easier for consumers to challenge unfair agreements and that the definition of 'extortionate' should be widened to cover unfair practices both at the time of entering the credit agreement as well as any subsequent events that may have led to unfairness"""'.

Detailed information has been provided to the 6 x Credit Card Companies
(NINE cards in total)

(MBNA Elyn Corfield - Capital One Amy Lenander - New Day Marbles Rob Holt - BarclayCard Chris Wood - RBS Marcellino Castrillo - New Day Opus - James Corcoran) who are known and are evidenced to practice Collateralised Credit Exploitation (CCE)

The Financial Conduct Authority Andrew Bailey - The Financial Ombudsman Caroline Wayman - The UK Cards Association Graham Peacop - The Prudential Regulation Authority Mark Carney - The Finance & Leasing Association Richard Jones - The British Bankers Association Eric Leenders - The Competition & Markets Authority Andrea Coscelli - The UK Parliament Phillip Hammond - The Lending & Standards Board Dave Pickering - The Payment Systems Regulator Hannah Nixon - The Money Advice Service Charles Counsell have been made fully aware of the practice of Collateralised Credit Exploitation (CCE).

EVERY Member of Parliament has victims of Collateralised Credit Exploitation in his or her constituency; suffering under the pain of unreasonable, unwarranted and unjustified behavior by Credit Card Companies.

British consumers have been slavishly providing extortionate, unjustified & unwarranted profits for Credit Card Companies for generations under the indefensibly false guise of 'long revolver credit' and are now holding them to account for their unwarranted financial profligacy of people's lives, their relationships, their income, their marriages & their life chances. Collateralised Credit Exploitation is entrapment & financial slavery

'Billions will be repaid to Millions' initial estimate of the cost to Credit Card Companies of Collateralised Credit Exploitation is conservatively put at between £50 - 75 Billion.

Exploitative By Design - Extortionate By Intent - Fraudulent By Nature

Never in the annals of financial history has so much been taken from so many by so few.

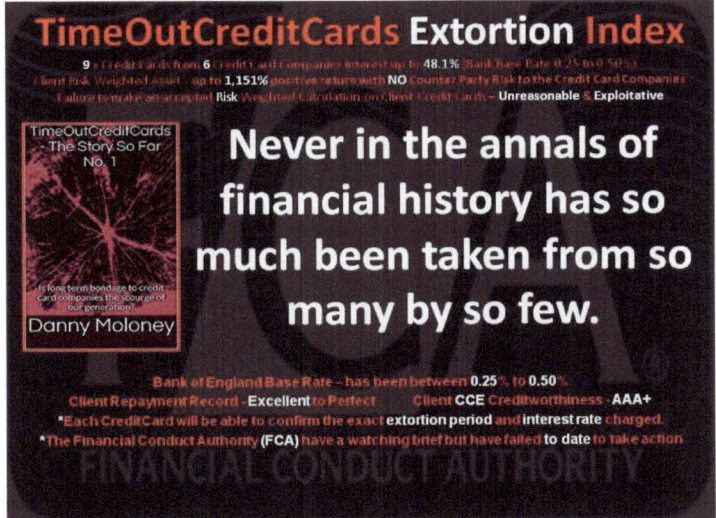

TimeOutCreditCards Collateralised Credit Exploitation: Never in the Annals of Financial History

TimeOutCreditCards Collateralised Credit Exploitation: Treating AAA+ Customers as Junk Accounts

TimeOutCreditCards Collateralised Credit Exploitation: REDlined Ending Financial Slavery

TimeOutCreditCards Collateralised Credit Exploitation: NO Risk BUT exploitative Rewards !!

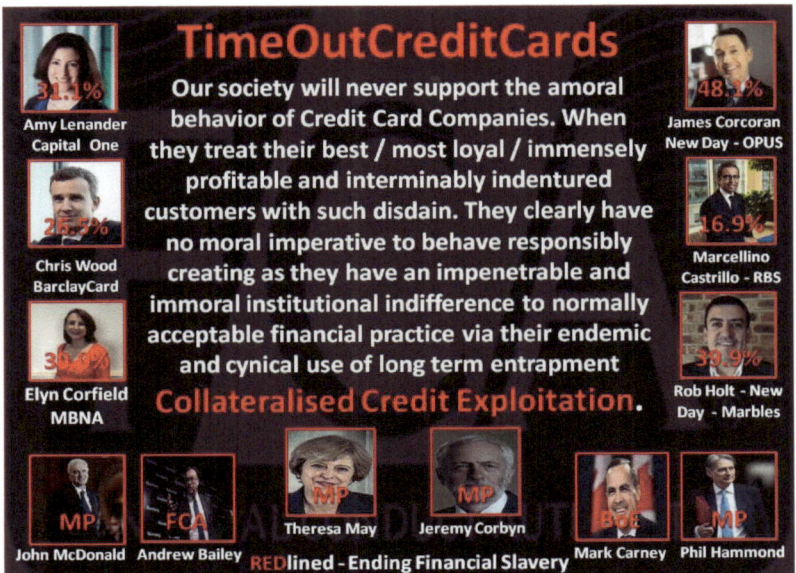

TimeOutCreditCards Collateralised Credit Exploitation: Cynical Use of Long Term Entrapment

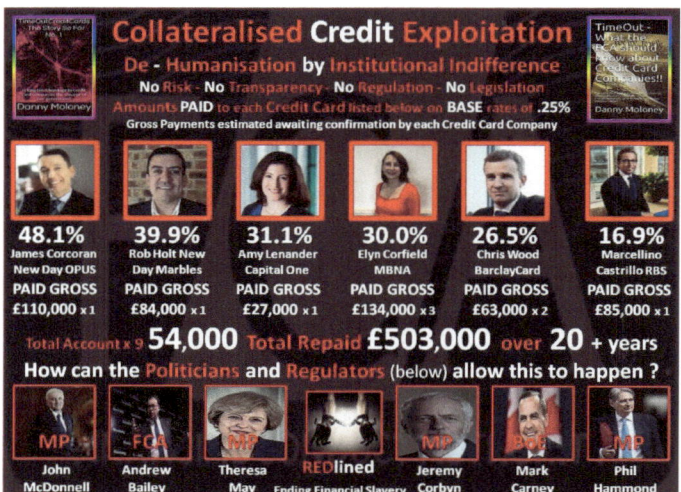

TimeOutCreditCards Collateralised Credit Exploitation: How can Legislators & Regulators allow this to happen?

TimeOutCreditCards Collateralised Credit Exploitation: It is NO surprise that there is NO response

TimeOutCreditCards Collateralised Credit Exploitation: Billions will be REPAID to millions

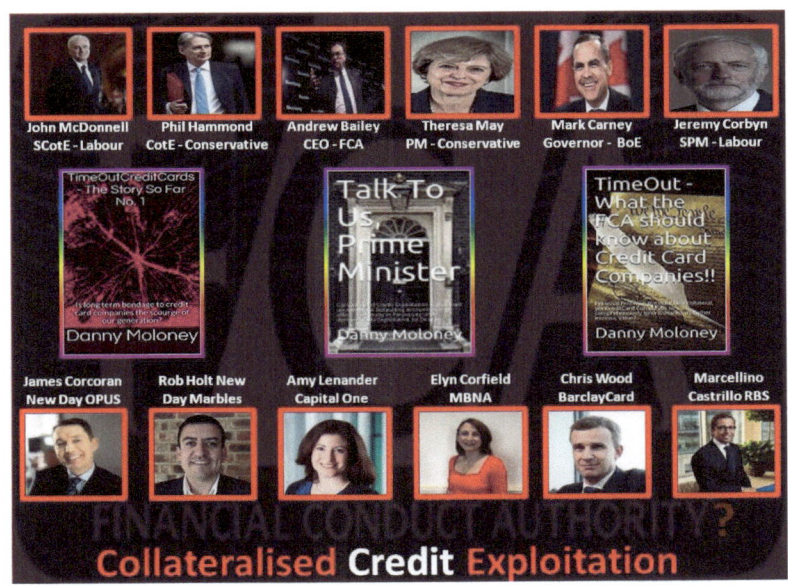

TimeOutCreditCards Collateralised Credit Exploitation: Talk to us, Prime Minister

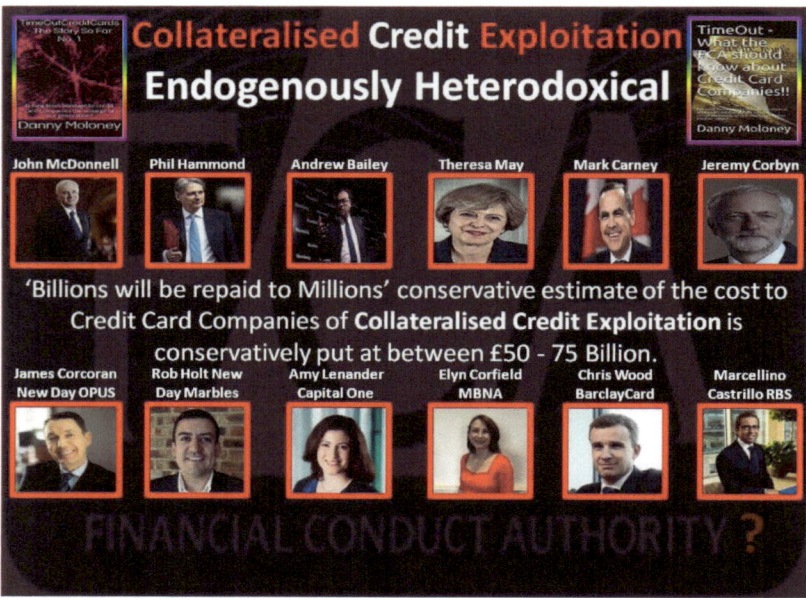

TimeOutCreditCards Collateralised Credit Exploitation: Endogenously Heterodoxical

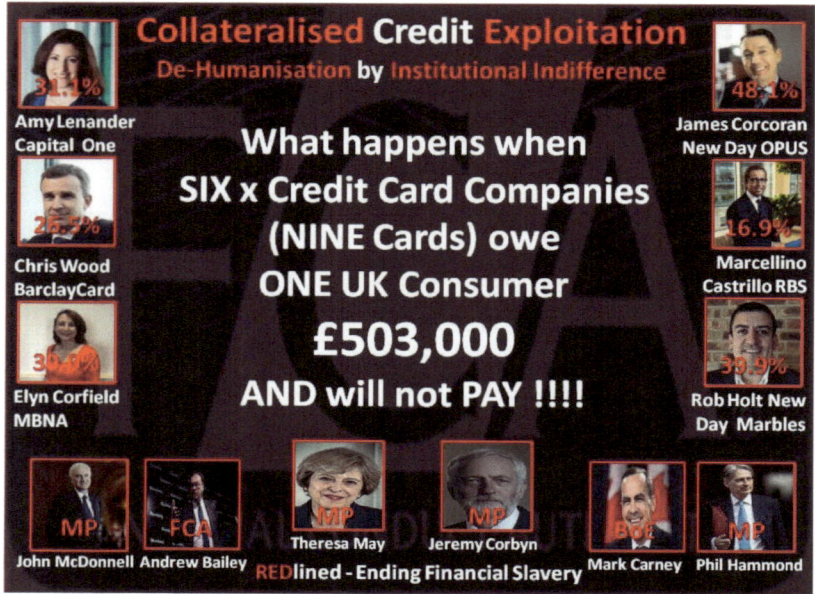

TimeOutCreditCards Collateralised Credit Exploitation: Should PAY, Won't PAY !!!

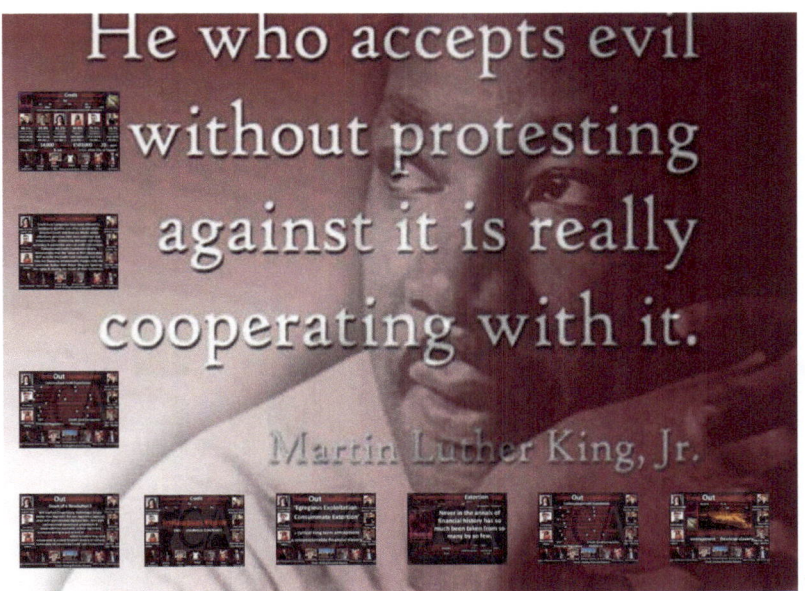

TimeOutCreditCards Collateralised Credit Exploitation: he Who Accepts Evil

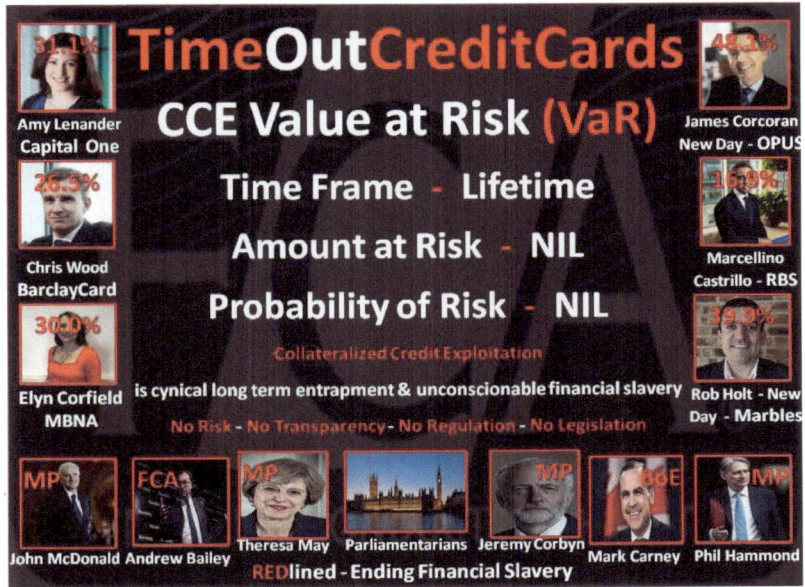

TimeOutCreditCards Collateralised Credit Exploitation: CCE Value AT Risk ?

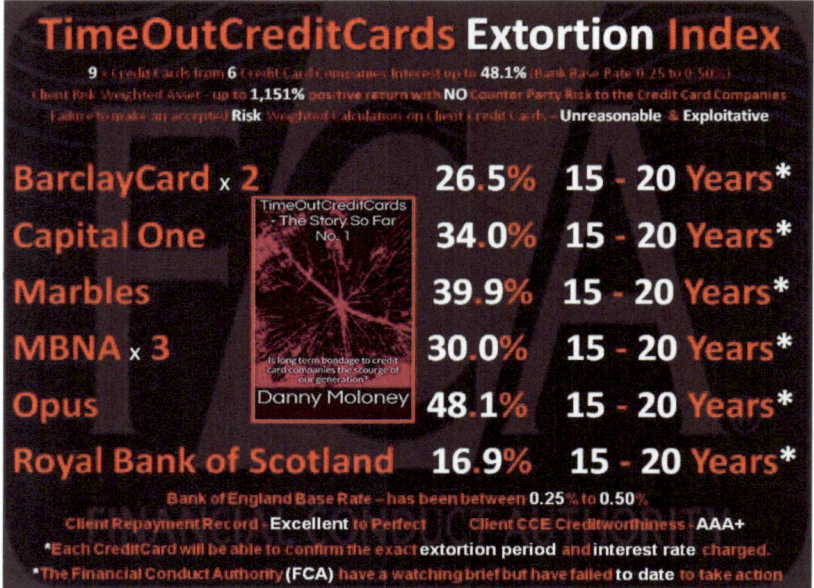

TimeOutCreditCards Collateralised Credit Exploitation: Extortion Index

TimeOutCreditCards Collateralised Credit Exploitation: PutAnEndToFinancialSlavery

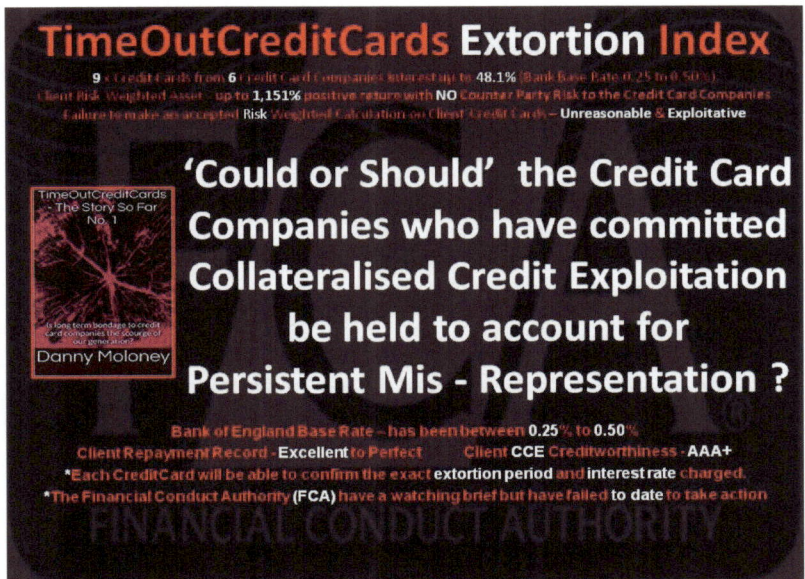

TimeOutCreditCards Collateralised Credit Exploitation: Could or Should

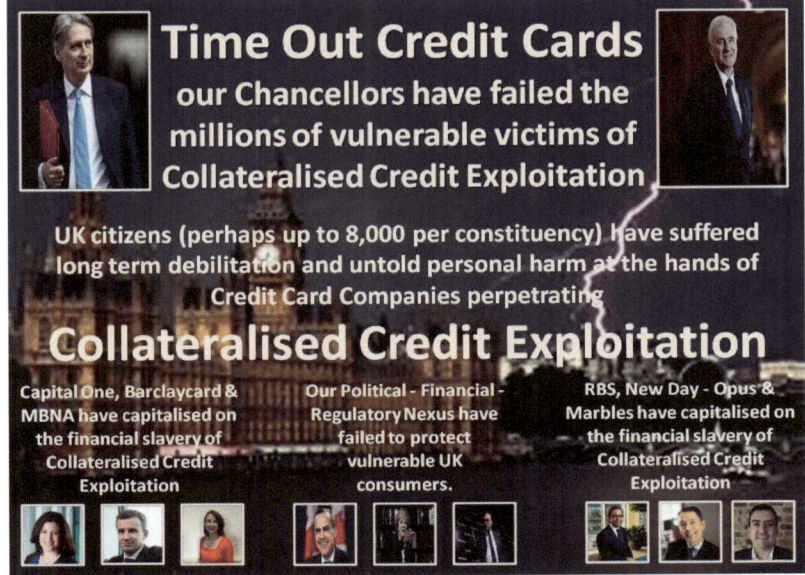

TimeOutCreditCards Collateralised Credit Exploitation: Our Chancellors have FAILED!!!

HomiGenesis Signature

Covering the birth, nurturing and early growth of the unique

'Homigenesis - An Uniquely Individual Male Perspective' philosophy

Encompassing and developing the following key concepts;

Individual - Empathic - Gregarious - Thoughtful - Appreciative – Holistic

Presented & promoted via a combination of 1) academic research papers and specially created business, 2) Case studies, popular published **3)** e-books & 4) p-books, 5) formal lectures, 6) informative seminars, 7) Knowledge exchange presentations, 8) keynote speeches and 9) consultancy & 10) coaching.

Hashtags

#Homigenesis,

#ecclesiast, #hominist, #individuateur, #PrintMediateur, #TechnoPreneur #Originateur,

Research Formats

Insights - Spotlights - Signposts - Pathways - Foresights - Scenarios – Opportunities

Jaeger (1,000)   Chronologs (2,000)   **Genesis (5,000)**
Essays (10,000)   Stories (20,000)   Novels & Theses (80,000)

Each containing a uniquely innovative 'Homigenesis Moment' for
Ecclesiast - Hominist - Individuateur - Originateur - PrintMediateur - TechnoPreneur

See also and keep in touch on

Ecclesiast
Acquiring & Developing Knowledge via Community - Culture -Creativity - EnterPrise.

Hominist
: Acquiring & Developing Knowledge via Masculinity - Man - Male - Manly -Manliness.

Individuateur
Acquiring & Developing Knowledge via Data - Information - Analysis - Knowledge.

Originateur
Acquiring & Developing Knowledge via Originality - Lifelong Learning -Transculturation – Innovation

PrintMediateur
Acquiring & Developing Knowledge via Channel - Media - Marketing - Print.

TechnoPreneur
Acquiring & Developing Knowledge via Capacity - Capability - Competence - Opportunity.

Sunday 22nd July 2018

Thank you for reading

Billions will be Repaid to Millions - Theresa May

""""It should be easier for consumers to challenge unfair agreements and that the definition of 'extortionate' should be widened to cover unfair practices both at the time of entering the credit agreement as well as any subsequent events that may have led to unfairness"""".

Part of GlobalMeHPTE, Greater Eccles, Manchester, United Kingdom.

Homigenesis

TechnoPreneur - Originateur - Hominist - Ecclesiast - Individuateur - Originateur

Tele: +44 7770 762860   Fax: + 44 161 789 8787

E-Mail: timeoutcreditcards@globalmehpte.com,

Words - 7,567   Images - 23   Pages - 40

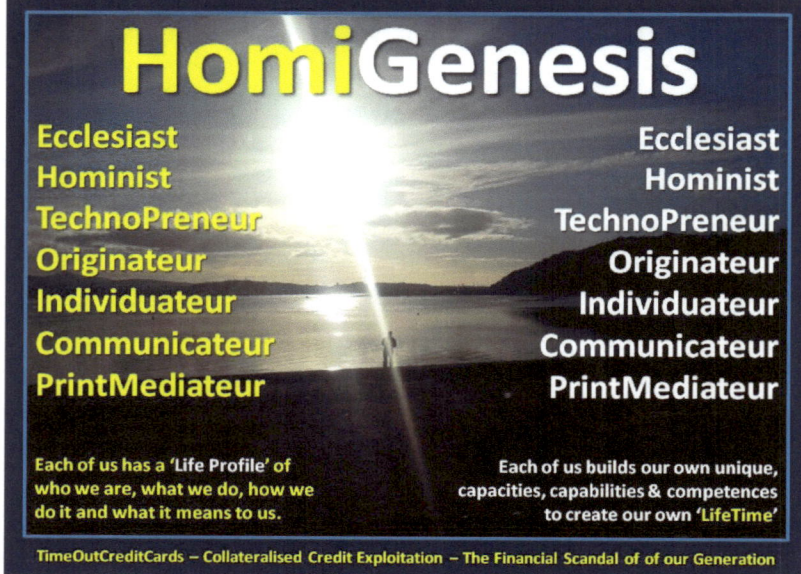

TimeOutCreditCards Collateralised Credit Exploitation – The Financial Scandal of our Generation

Financial Slavery by Credit Card Companies

No financial organization has the right to make excessive interest & charges on nominal amounts that cannot be paid back within an individual's lifetime.

www.ingramcontent.com/pod-product-compliance
Lightning Source LLC
Chambersburg PA
CBHW040335220526
45473CB00009B/2687